SMART ABOUT
History

SMART ABOUT THE

FIFTY STATES

Written and illustrated by
Jon Buller & Susan Schade, Maryann Cocca-Leffler,
Joan Holub, True Kelley, and Dana Regan

Grosset & Dunlap
An Imprint of Penguin Group (USA) Inc.

W9-CAG-790

Delron's pages by Jon Buller & Susan Schade.
Tori's pages by Maryann Cocca-Leffler.
Nick's pages by Joan Holub.
Jamaica's pages by True Kelley.
Joe's pages by Dana Regan.

Copyright © 2003 by Jon Buller & Susan Schade, copyright © 2003 by Maryann Cocca-Leffler, copyright © 2003 by Joan Holub, copyright © 2003 by True Kelley, copyright © 2003, 2013 by Dana Regan. All rights reserved. Published by Grosset & Dunlap, a division of Penguin Young Readers Group, 345 Hudson Street, New York, NY 10014. GROSSET & DUNLAP is a trademark of Penguin Group (USA) Inc. Published simultaneously in Canada. Manufactured in China.

Library of Congress Control Number: 2003005961

ISBN 978-0-448-43131-4   17 18 19 20

ALWAYS LEARNING   PEARSON

Dear Class,

    I am so eager to see your group reports. I hope that working together with classmates will be lots of fun. It's very different from doing a report all by yourself, isn't it?

    First your group needs to pick a subject. Then you must figure out a way to divide the work fairly. And <u>then</u> you have to put the whole report together.

    This is not an easy assignment. But I know that you will all do a GREAT job!

               Ms. Brandt

ABOUT THIS REPORT

Dear Ms. Brandt,

   Here is our class report. It is on the fifty states. There were five kids in our group. We each picked a different part of the country to write about.

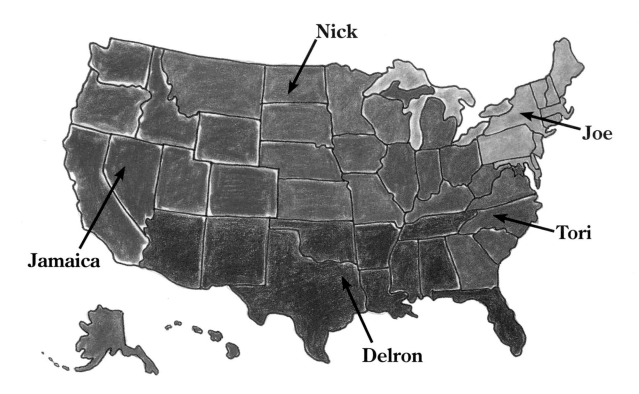

   Our computer teacher helped us make a worksheet for each state. You can see who did each page, because we signed our names at the bottom. This was fun. We had a pizza party when we were all done!

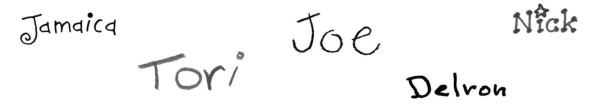

TABLE OF CONTENTS

The United

Washington
Oregon
Montana
North Dakota
South Dakota
Idaho
Wyoming
Nebraska
Nevada
California
Utah
Colorado
Kansas
Pacific Ocean
Arizona
New Mexico
Oklahoma
Texas
Alaska
Hawaii

State  **ALABAMA**

Its nickname is _Cotton State_

Its capital is _Montgomery_

BOLL WEEVILS (COTTON PEST)

HUNTSVILLE: U.S. SPACE AND ROCKET CENTER

TALLADEGA SUPERSPEEDWAY

MOUNDVILLE (PREHISTORIC MOUND VILLAGE)

MONTGOMERY

CAPITOL BUILDING

PRODUCTS: COAL, PAPER, IRON, STEEL

MOBILE

TUSKEGEE INSTITUTE

SEAFOOD JUBILEE (LATE SUMMER)

WHERE GEORGE WASHINGTON CARVER DISCOVERED OVER 300 NEW USES FOR THE PEANUT.

FAMOUS PERSON

IN 1955, ROSA PARKS GOT ARRESTED FOR REFUSING TO GIVE UP HER SEAT IN A BUS TO A WHITE PERSON. HER ARREST LED TO PROTESTS AND IMPORTANT VICTORIES IN THE CIVIL RIGHTS MOVEMENT.

Alabama has a lot of cool caves—one had ten-thousand-year-old human bones in it! Alabama is also where some of the most important victories of the Civil Rights Movement took place, such as the Montgomery bus boycott of 1955. The Civil Rights Act of 1964 says you can't discriminate because of color, race, national origin, religion, or sex. That's a great law!

This great state has been brought to you by _Delron Moore_

ALASKA

State _____

Its nickname is **The Last Frontier**

Its capital is **Juneau** (Say it like this: Jū-nō.)

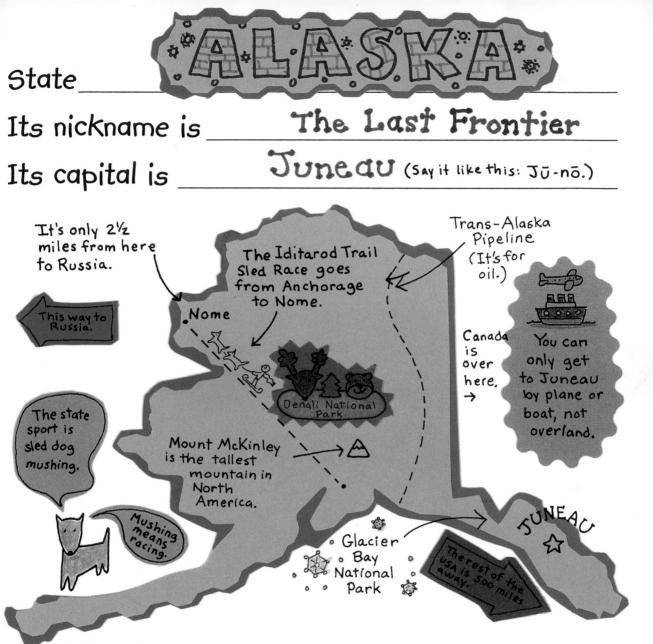

It's only 2½ miles from here to Russia.

This way to Russia.

The Iditarod Trail Sled Race goes from Anchorage to Nome.

Nome

Denali National Park

The state sport is sled dog mushing.

Mount McKinley is the tallest mountain in North America.

Mushing means racing.

Trans-Alaska Pipeline (It's for oil.)

Canada is over here. →

You can only get to Juneau by plane or boat, not overland.

JUNEAU

Glacier Bay National Park

The rest of the USA is 500 miles away.

Alaska is the biggest state. It's twice as big as Texas. But it doesn't have that many people. Why? Probably because it's cold! Once it got as cold as 79.8 degrees F below zero. *Brrr!* I thought lots of people in Alaska lived in igloos. Nope! Most of them live in houses or apartments (like me). The U.S. bought Alaska from Russia in 1867 for only two cents an acre. People thought it was a bad deal for the U.S. at the time. Were they wrong! Alaska is rich in oil and fish. And it's beautiful, too.

This great state has been brought to you by **Nick Nation**

State **ARIZONA**

Its nickname is _Grand Canyon State_

Its capital is _Phoenix_

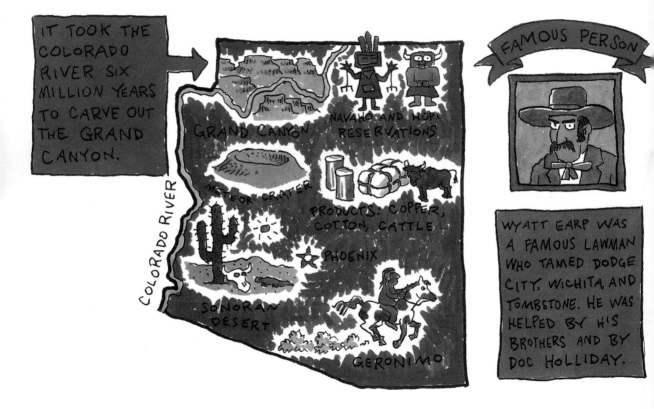

IT TOOK THE COLORADO RIVER SIX MILLION YEARS TO CARVE OUT THE GRAND CANYON.

GRAND CANYON

COLORADO RIVER

METEOR CRATER

SONORAN DESERT

NAVAHO AND HOPI RESERVATIONS

PRODUCTS: COPPER, COTTON, CATTLE

PHOENIX

GERONIMO

FAMOUS PERSON

WYATT EARP WAS A FAMOUS LAWMAN WHO TAMED DODGE CITY, WICHITA AND TOMBSTONE. HE WAS HELPED BY HIS BROTHERS AND BY DOC HOLLIDAY.

Tools and weapons found in Arizona show that people lived there at least 12,000 years ago. In the 1500s Spanish explorers came to Arizona looking for "Cities of Gold." They never found any. But in 1858 prospectors found gold at Gila City. Some of the mining "boomtowns" that prospectors built are now deserted ghost towns. Cool!

This great state has been brought to you by _Delron Moore_

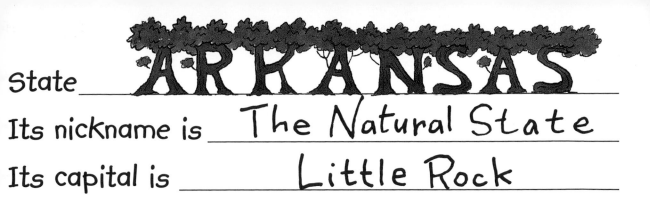

State **ARKANSAS**

Its nickname is **The Natural State**

Its capital is **Little Rock**

Arkansas is pronounced AR-ken-saw. People who live there are called Arkansans, which is pronounced ar-KAN-zens. Go figure! Arkansans are famous for telling tall tales. They like folk music and have kitchen bands that play music on pots and pans and washtubs. I think Arkansas sounds like a fun state.

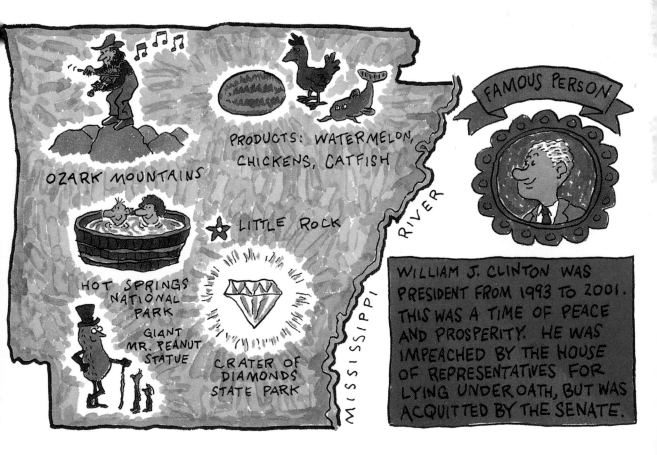

OZARK MOUNTAINS

PRODUCTS: WATERMELON, CHICKENS, CATFISH

LITTLE ROCK

HOT SPRINGS NATIONAL PARK

GIANT MR. PEANUT STATUE

CRATER OF DIAMONDS STATE PARK

MISSISSIPPI RIVER

FAMOUS PERSON

WILLIAM J. CLINTON WAS PRESIDENT FROM 1993 TO 2001. THIS WAS A TIME OF PEACE AND PROSPERITY. HE WAS IMPEACHED BY THE HOUSE OF REPRESENTATIVES FOR LYING UNDER OATH, BUT WAS ACQUITTED BY THE SENATE.

This great state has been brought to you by **Delron Moore**

State **CALIFORNIA**

Its nickname is _The Golden State_

Its capital is _SACRAMENTO_

California's got everything! There are snowcapped mountains, beaches, farms, vineyards, deserts, big cities, redwood forests . . . and of course, there's Hollywood and Disneyland! I guess that's why more people live in California than in any other state. (I might be nervous living there because of the earthquakes.) California grows the most food in the U.S. . . . over half of all U.S. fruits and veggies. California oranges. Yum!

This great state has been brought to you by _Jamaica King_

State **COLORADO**

Its nickname is __The Centennial State__

Its capital is __DENVER__ ↖ it became a state on the 100th birthday of the U.S.

Colorado has more high mountains than any other state. The skiing and snowboarding are awesome! *Tyrannosaurus rex* fossils have been found in Colorado, and, in the 1970s, two of the biggest dinosaur skeletons were dug up near Grand Junction.

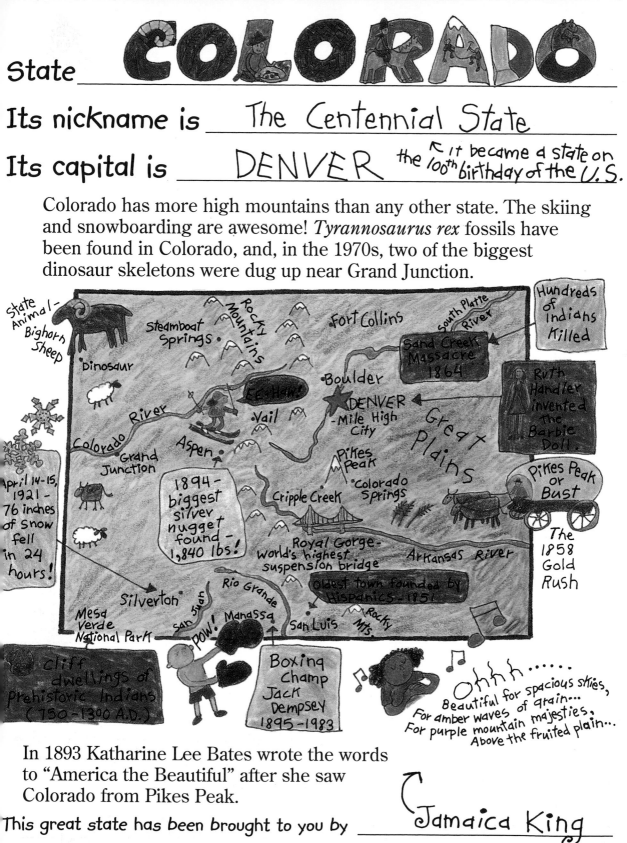

State Animal - Bighorn Sheep

Steamboat Springs

Rocky Mountains

Fort Collins

South Platte River

Sand Creek Massacre 1864

Hundreds of Indians Killed

Dinosaur

EE-HAW!

Boulder

DENVER - Mile High City

Great Plains

Ruth Handler invented the Barbie Doll.

Colorado River

Vail

Aspen

Grand Junction

April 14-15, 1921 - 76 inches of snow fell in 24 hours!

1894 - biggest silver nugget found - 1,840 lbs!

Cripple Creek

Pikes Peak

Colorado Springs

Pikes Peak or Bust

Royal Gorge - world's highest suspension bridge

Arkansas River

The 1858 Gold Rush

Silverton

Rio Grande

San Juan

POW! Manassa

San Luis

Rocky Mts.

Oldest town founded by Hispanics - 1851

Mesa Verde National Park

Cliff dwellings of Prehistoric Indians (750-1300 A.D.)

Boxing Champ Jack Dempsey 1895-1983

Ohhh......
Beautiful for spacious skies,
For amber waves of grain...
For purple mountain majesties,
Above the fruited plain...

In 1893 Katharine Lee Bates wrote the words to "America the Beautiful" after she saw Colorado from Pikes Peak.

This great state has been brought to you by __Jamaica King__

13

State **Connecticut**

Its nickname is _The Constitution State or the Nutmeg State_

Its capital is _Hartford_

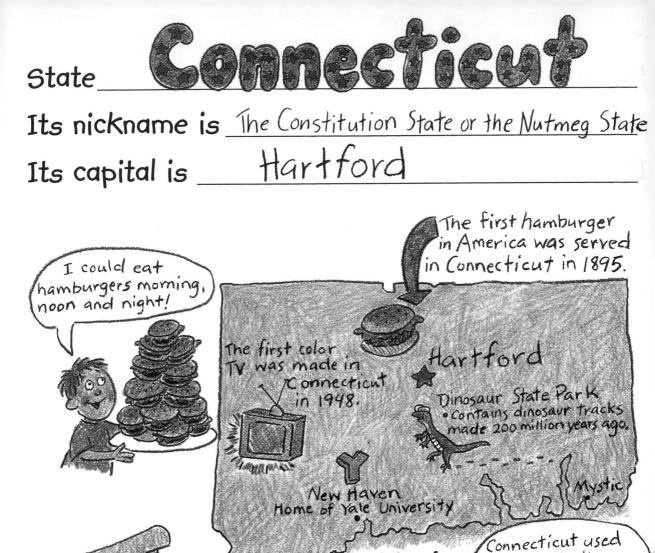

The first hamburger in America was served in Connecticut in 1895.

I could eat hamburgers morning, noon and night!

The first color TV was made in Connecticut in 1948.

Hartford

Dinosaur State Park
• Contains dinosaur tracks made 200 million years ago.

New Haven
Home of Yale University

Mystic

Connecticut used to be a whaling center. Now whales are protected.

Connecticut was one of the original thirteen states. Are you wondering why it's called the Constitution State when the U.S. Constitution was written in Philadelphia? When Connecticut was still a colony, it was the first place to write up laws and rules—and that's what a constitution is.

This great state has been brought to you by _Joe_

14

State

Its nickname is ___The First State___

Its capital is ___Dover___

Delaware was the very first state to join the Union in 1787. It is named after Baron De La Warr, who was the first governor of the Virginia colony, and who sent explorers along the coast of Delaware. Delaware's coast is mostly swamps and marshlands and is a stopover for migrating ducks and geese. There are also lots of horseshoe crabs on the beaches. Horseshoe crabs can go a year without eating. They look basically the same as they did back in the days of the dinosaurs.

The ladybug is the state bug.

Delaware is known for its delicious seafood.

Delaware River

Dover

← Horseshoe crab

The first log cabins in the U.S. were built in Delaware.

This great state has been brought to you by ___Joe___

State **FLORIDA**

Its nickname is _Sunshine State_

Its capital is _Tallahassee_

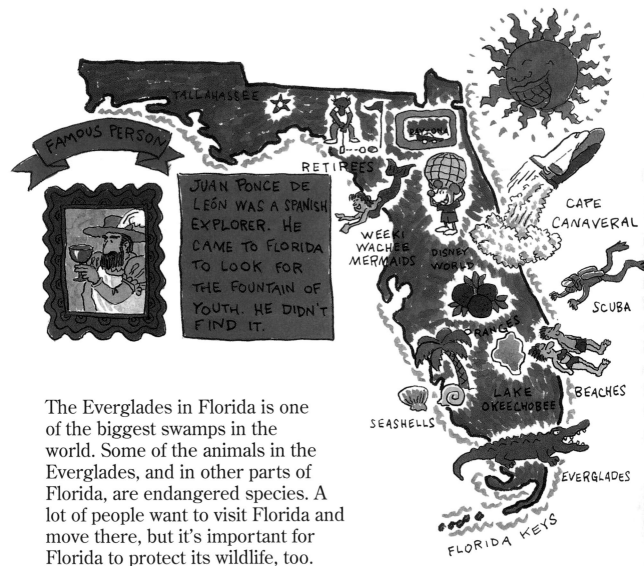

FAMOUS PERSON

JUAN PONCE DE LEÓN WAS A SPANISH EXPLORER. HE CAME TO FLORIDA TO LOOK FOR THE FOUNTAIN OF YOUTH. HE DIDN'T FIND IT.

TALLAHASSEE

RETIREES

DAYTONA

WEEKI WACHEE MERMAIDS

DISNEY WORLD

CAPE CANAVERAL

SCUBA

ORANGES

LAKE OKEECHOBEE

SEASHELLS

BEACHES

EVERGLADES

FLORIDA KEYS

The Everglades in Florida is one of the biggest swamps in the world. Some of the animals in the Everglades, and in other parts of Florida, are endangered species. A lot of people want to visit Florida and move there, but it's important for Florida to protect its wildlife, too.

This great state has been brought to you by _Delron Moore_

State **Georgia**

Its nickname is **The Peach State**

Its capital is **Atlanta**

White Gold!

Lots of **COTTON** is grown in Georgia! Eli Whitney invented the cotton gin in 1793. It was a machine that separated the seeds from the cotton. (Before that, seeds had to be picked out by hand!) The cotton gin saved lots of time.

Coca-Cola was invented here in 1886!

Atlanta

Our thirtyninth president, Jimmy Carter, and Martin Luther King, Jr. were born in Georgia.

Savannah

• Cairo

FUN FACT

Half of all the peanuts grown in the U.S. come from Georgia.

Peanut Butter is born!

In 1890 a storekeeper ground some peanuts up and began selling his "nut butter" for six cents a pound. I LOVE peanut butter!

Atlantic Ocean

1ST

In 1947, Jackie Robinson, from Cairo, was the first black person to play professional baseball in the twentieth century.

This great state has been brought to you by **Tori**

State  _____

Gecko lizard brings good luck!

Its nickname is _The Aloha State_ ← *Aloha means "love", "hello" and "goodbye".*

Its capital is ___Honolulu___

Hawaii is the only state made up entirely of islands. (There are 132 so I just put the big ones on my map.) From Hawaii we get pineapples, sugar, macadamia nuts, and crazy Hawaiian shirts.

KAUAI - The Garden Island

Mt. Waialeale: The wettest place on earth! 460"+ rain per year!

OAHU - The Gathering Place (Most Hawaiians live here.)

Pearl Harbor

Honolulu

Leatherback Turtles - world's biggest sea turtles

WOW!

me

U.S. Mainland 2,000 miles

MOLOKAI - The Friendly Island

World's highest sea cliffs

LANAI - The Pineapple Island

MAUI - The Valley Island

Haleakala - World's biggest dormant volcano.

HULA!

~ Lei

Hawaiians invented surfing in ancient times. It's America's oldest sport.

Parker Ranch Biggest in U.S.

HAWAII - The Big Island

Mauna Kia Volcano

Hilo

orchids!

Kilauea world's most active volcano

Mauna Loa Volcano

Ka Lae, the southernmost place in the U.S.!

My favorite author, Lois Lowry, is from Hawaii. Hawaii sounds so cool—kids can go to school barefoot! But some sad things have happened there. In 1941 the Japanese attacked Pearl Harbor. This made the U.S. start fighting in World War II.

"Mahalo" (thank yo

This great state has been brought to you by _____ Jamaica King

State **IDAHO**

Its nickname is **The Gem State ; The Spud State**
←(more than 80 kinds!)
Its capital is **BOISE**

At the supermarket, you'll probably see Idaho potatoes.
Idaho grows one-third of all the potatoes in the U.S.

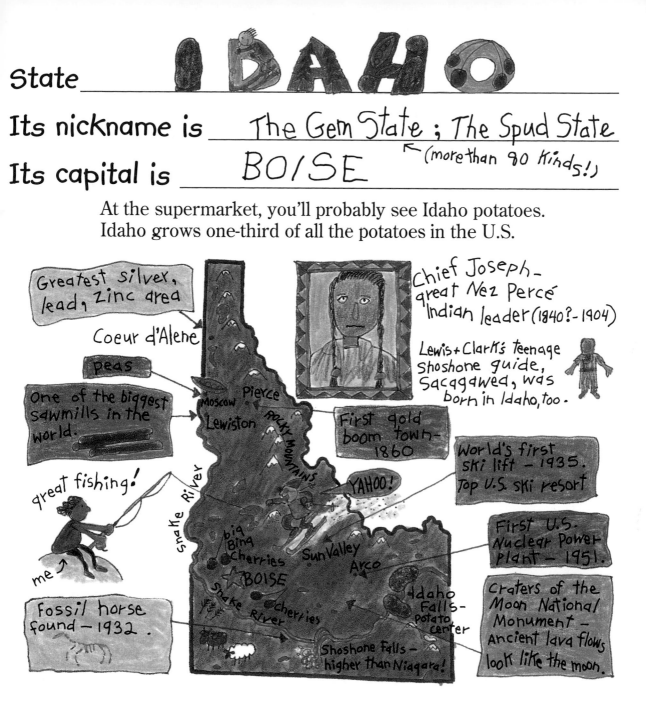

Greatest silver, lead, zinc area

Coeur d'Alene

peas

One of the biggest sawmills in the world.

great fishing!

me →

Fossil horse found — 1932.

Moscow   Pierce
Lewiston   ROCKY MOUNTAINS
Snake River

big Bing Cherries   Sun Valley   Arco
BOISE
Shake River   Cherries
Idaho Falls - potato center

Shoshone Falls — higher than Niagara!

YAHOO!

Chief Joseph - great Nez Percé Indian leader (1840? - 1904)

Lewis + Clark's teenage Shoshone guide, Sacagawea, was born in Idaho, too.

First gold boom town — 1860

World's first ski lift — 1935. Top U.S. ski resort

First U.S. Nuclear Power Plant — 1951.

Craters of the Moon National Monument — Ancient lava flows look like the moon.

If you like to go rock hunting, Idaho's the place for you. It's also great for outdoor stuff—hiking, biking, hunting, fishing, skiing, river rafting! There are so many lakes, hundreds are still unexplored! There are also 81 mountain ranges! I read that if it was rolled out flat, Idaho would be as big as Texas.

This great state has been brought to you by _____ **Jamaica King**

State **ILLINOIS**

Its nickname is _Prairie State_

Its capital is _Springfield_

Illinois is as flat as a pancake with lots of prairies.

"A house divided against itself cannot stand."

Before cars, people traveled by stagecoach. You can still do it on the Stagecoach Trail.

Chicago

The world's first and biggest Ferris wheel was invented by George Ferris and thrilled the nation at the Chicago World's Fair in 1893.

Springfield

The Willis Tower in Chicago is the tallest building in the U.S.

FUN FACT

Abe Lincoln spent most of his life in Illinois. Lincoln was against slavery. In 1858 he made a famous speech that got the attention of the country. He went on to become our sixteenth president.

In 1837, John Deere, a blacksmith, invented a new steel plow that made it easier for farmers to turn prairie land, which was filled with tangled roots, into farmland.

This great state has been brought to you by _Tori_

State **Indiana**

Its nickname is **The Hoosier State**

Its capital is **Indianapolis**

"Who's Yere?"

Fort Wayne

1ST

The first professional-league game of baseball was played in Fort Wayne on May 4, 1871.

Hoosiers is the nickname for people who live in Indiana. Some say the name comes from pioneer days when a person answered the door asking, "Who's yere?"

Indianapolis

FUN FACT

Indiana means "land of Indians"

There is a town called Santa Claus, and it gets a lot of mail every Christmas.

Santa Claus

The **Indy 500** is a famous international car race that takes place every Memorial Day weekend. The first race was on May 30, 1911. The cars go 500 miles (200 laps) around the Indianapolis Motor Speedway.

This great state has been brought to you by ___**Tori**___

State **IOWA** zzz ← The name comes from a Dakota Native American word that means "the sleepy ones."

Its nickname is _The Hawkeye State_

Its capital is _Des Moines_ (Say it like this: Duh Moyn.)

What has 195 huge dirt mounds, including 31 built in bird and bear shapes? Answer: The Effigy Mounds National Monument in Iowa. The dirt mounds are Native American graves. The Great Bear is 137 feet long!

Sioux City has the biggest popcorn factory in the USA!

The Effigy Mounds National Monument is here.

An artist named Grant Wood had an art school here in Stone City. His most famous painting was of a farmer and his wife. It was called "American Gothic."

DES MOINES ← The capital and biggest city.

The Iowa State Fair in Des Moines lasts eleven days.

Every August, the Iowa State Fair is held. It's like a party to celebrate farming and ranching because farms cover 90% of Iowa. There are carnival rides and a hog-calling contest. The fair is so famous that three movies have been made about it.

This great state has been brought to you by _Nick Nation_

22

State **KANSAS**

Its nickname is The Sunflower State

Its capital is Topeka

Amelia Earhart was born in Atchison, Kansas. She was the first woman ever to fly over the Atlantic Ocean all alone.

Atchison

Kansas City

Lebanon is the geographical center of the lower 48 states.

The Barbed Wire Museum in LaCrosse has 2,000 kinds of barbed wire.

TOPEKA

Dodge City was once a famous Wild West town.

Wyatt Earp was the sheriff of Dodge City.

Wichita is the biggest city in Kansas.

Liberal

In Liberal, you can visit a house made to look like Dorothy's house in "The Wizard of Oz" movie.

Nation's Breadbasket

Kansas grows more wheat than any other state, so it's called the "Nation's Breadbasket." Kansas farms also grow popcorn, sunflower seeds, and soybeans. Kansas has another nickname: Tornado Alley. The biggest tornado in the U.S. was in Kansas in 1947. Dorothy from L. Frank Baum's *The Wonderful Wizard of Oz* lived on a farm in Kansas.

This great state has been brought to you by ___Nick Nation

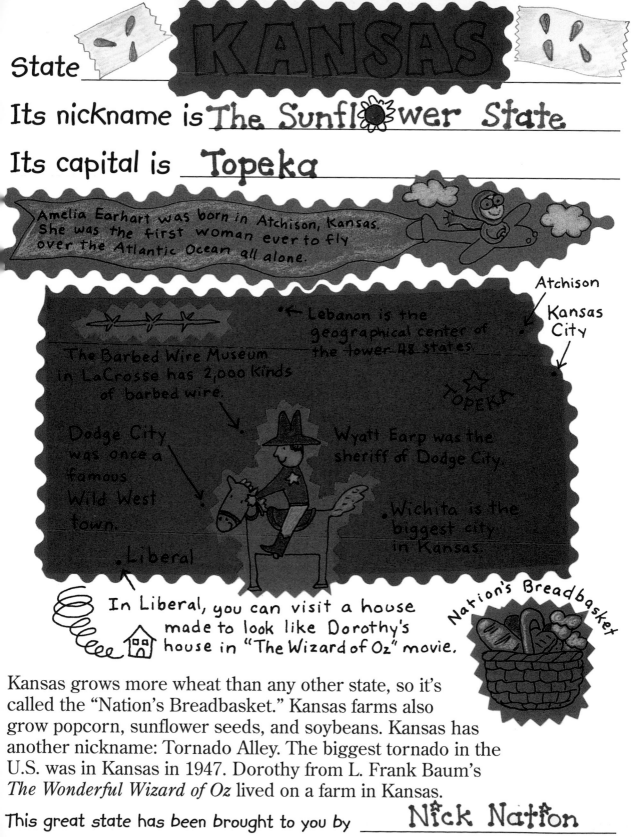

23

State **KENTUCKY**

Its nickname is **Bluegrass State**

Its capital is **Frankfort**

Bluegrass isn't really blue. It's green. Blue flowers that bloom in May give it a bluish tint.

FUN FACT

1ST

The Kentucky Derby was first run in 1875. It is a famous thoroughbred horse race that takes place every May, lasting about two minutes!

In 1775, explorer Daniel Boone led the first white settlers into Kentucky. In 1776, his daughter was captured by Shawnee. She tore off bits of her dress and tied them to branches. Her father followed her trail and rescued her. Later, Daniel Boone became friends with the Native Americans.

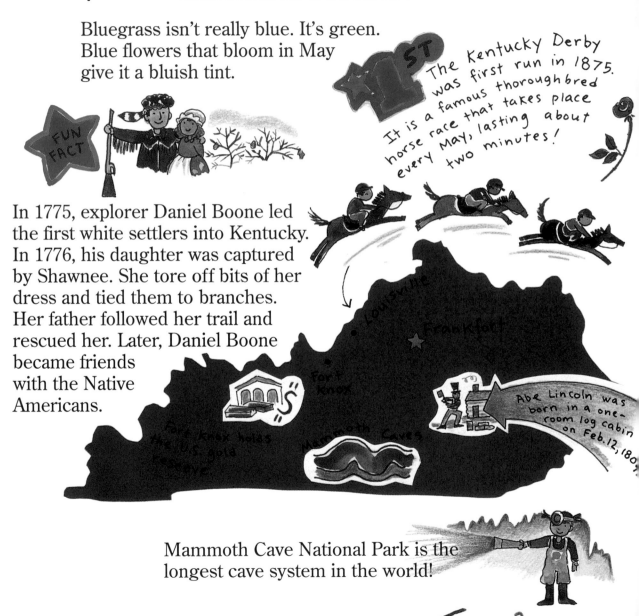

Louisville

Frankfort

Fort Knox

Fort Knox holds the U.S. gold Reserve

Mammoth Caves

Abe Lincoln was born in a one-room log cabin on Feb. 12, 180?

Mammoth Cave National Park is the longest cave system in the world!

Tori

This great state has been brought to you by _____

State  **LOUISIANA**

Its nickname is **Pelican State**

Its capital is **Baton Rouge**

In Louisiana, there are special names for lots of stuff. Bayou—
pronounced BY-yoo—means a marshy, slow-moving stream.
Jambalaya—pronounced jum-buh-LIE-yuh—is a spicy rice dish.
Baton Rouge—pronounced BATT-in ROOJ—is the state capital. It is
French for "red stick." Mardi Gras—pronounced MAR-dee GRAH—
is a big festival. It's French for "fat Tuesday."

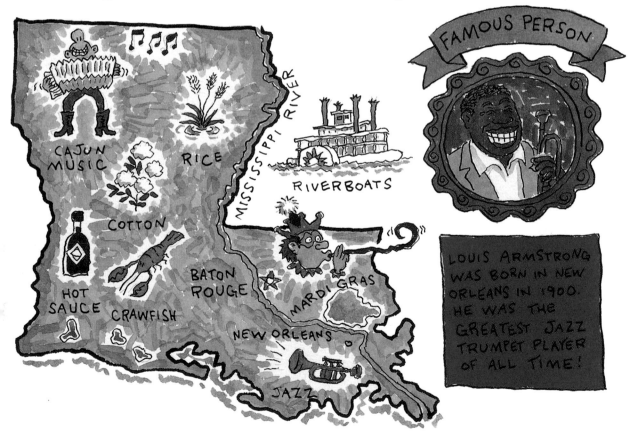

CAJUN MUSIC

RICE

MISSISSIPPI RIVER

RIVERBOATS

COTTON

HOT SAUCE

CRAWFISH

BATON ROUGE

MARDI GRAS

NEW ORLEANS

JAZZ

FAMOUS PERSON

LOUIS ARMSTRONG WAS BORN IN NEW ORLEANS IN 1900. HE WAS THE GREATEST JAZZ TRUMPET PLAYER OF ALL TIME!

This great state has been brought to you by **Delron Moore**

State **MAINE**

Its nickname is _The Pine Tree State_

Its capital is _Augusta_

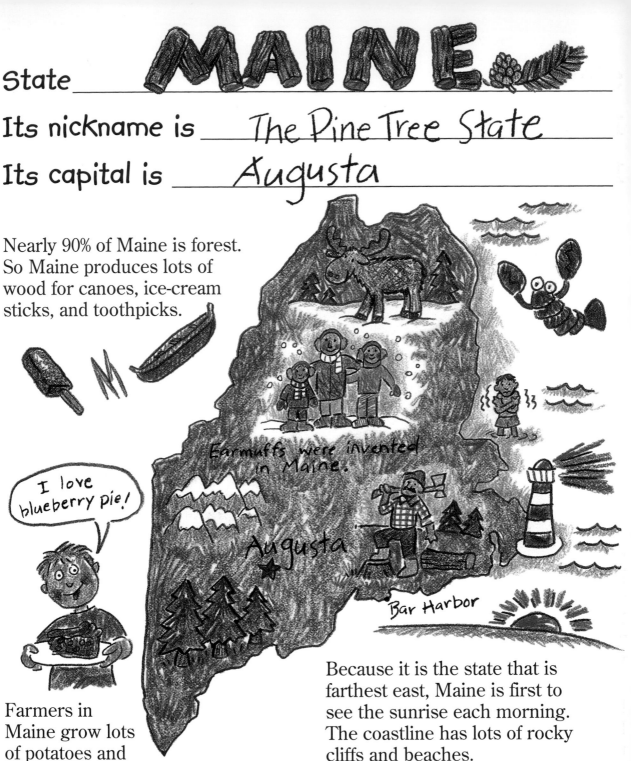

Nearly 90% of Maine is forest. So Maine produces lots of wood for canoes, ice-cream sticks, and toothpicks.

Earmuffs were invented in Maine.

I love blueberry pie!

Augusta

Bar Harbor

Farmers in Maine grow lots of potatoes and blueberries. Yum!

Because it is the state that is farthest east, Maine is first to see the sunrise each morning. The coastline has lots of rocky cliffs and beaches.

This great state has been brought to you by _Joe_

State __Maryland__

Its nickname is __The Free State or Old Line State__

Its capital is __Annapolis__

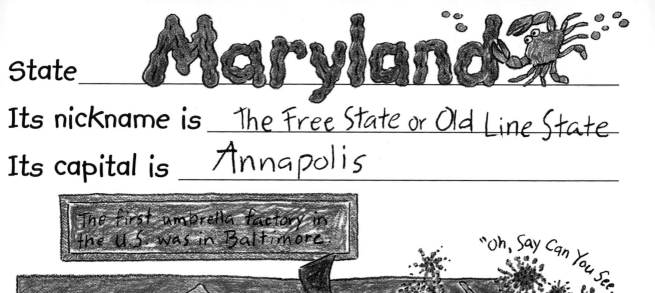

The first umbrella factory in the U.S. was in Baltimore.

"Oh, Say Can You See..."

Baltimore
Fort McHenry
Annapolis
Chesapeake Bay

U.S. Naval Academy

Our national anthem, "The Star-Spangled Banner," was written by Francis Scott Key while he watched the British bomb Fort McHenry in Baltimore Harbor. That was during the War of 1812. We won!

Maryland surrounds the Chesapeake Bay, which produces more blue crabs than anywhere else in the country. (Lots of oysters, too!)

I've never eaten a crab before.

This great state has been brought to you by ___Joe___

State **Massachusetts**

Its nickname is _Bay State or Old Colony State_

Its capital is _Boston_

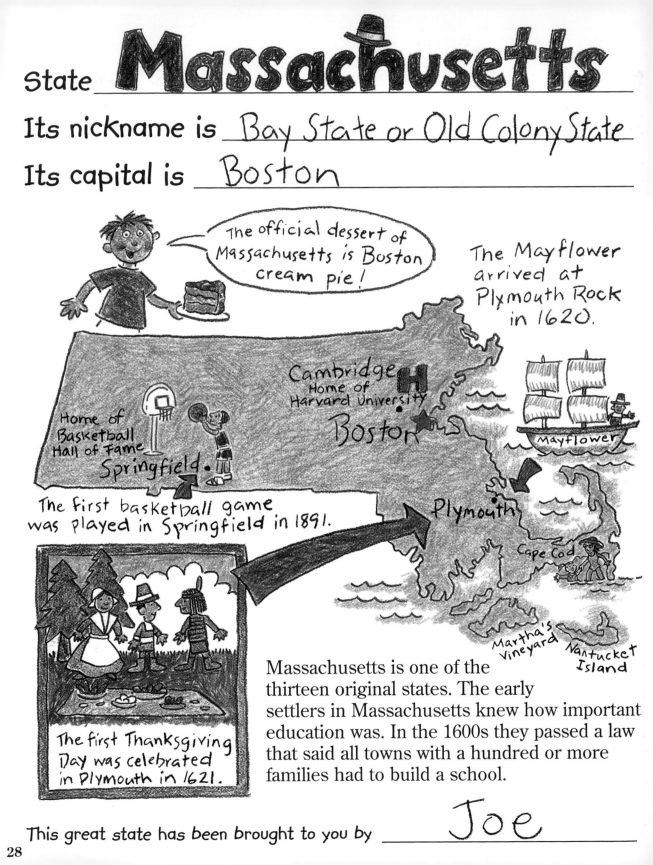

The official dessert of Massachusetts is Boston cream pie!

The Mayflower arrived at Plymouth Rock in 1620.

Cambridge
Home of Harvard University

Boston

Mayflower

Home of Basketball Hall of Fame
Springfield

The first basketball game was played in Springfield in 1891.

Plymouth

Cape Cod

Martha's Vineyard   Nantucket Island

The first Thanksgiving Day was celebrated in Plymouth in 1621.

Massachusetts is one of the thirteen original states. The early settlers in Massachusetts knew how important education was. In the 1600s they passed a law that said all towns with a hundred or more families had to build a school.

This great state has been brought to you by _Joe_

State **Michigan**

Its nickname is __Great Lakes State__

Its capital is __Lansing__

Isle Royale →

Lake Superior

Four of the five Great Lakes surround Michigan. It has 3,288 miles of shoreline. It is the only state divided into two parts, the Upper Peninsula and Lower Peninsula.

Upper Peninsula

The Mackinac Bridge connects the two peninsulas.

#1ST In U.S. Henry Ford and Ransom E. Olds made the first gasoline-powered cars in 1896.

The Sleeping Bear Dunes are hundreds of acres of big sandpiles. One dune looks like a giant bear. →

Lower Peninsula

The Lower Peninsula is shaped like a mitten!

Yum!

FUN FACT

Lake Michigan

Lake Huron

Lots of cars are made here

Lansing

Battle Creek is home to the Post and Kellogg's companies. Charles Post invented "Postum," one of the first breakfast cereals . . . John and William Kellogg invented the first corn flakes!

Detroit

Battle Creek

Lake Erie

This great state has been brought to you by __Tori__

State _____ **MINNESOTA**

Its nickname is _The Gopher State_

Its capital is _St. Paul_

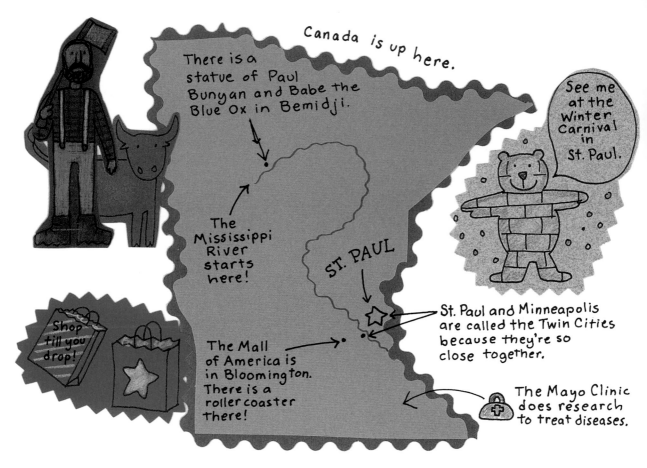

Canada is up here.

There is a statue of Paul Bunyan and Babe the Blue Ox in Bemidji.

The Mississippi River starts here!

See me at the Winter Carnival in St. Paul.

ST. PAUL

St. Paul and Minneapolis are called the Twin Cities because they're so close together.

Shop till you drop!

The Mall of America is in Bloomington. There is a roller coaster there!

The Mayo Clinic does research to treat diseases.

Minnesota is sometimes called the Land of 10,000 Lakes. But there are really more than 15,000 lakes there. I think Minnesota could be nicknamed the Land of Shopping. The Mall of America in Bloomington has over 400 stores! Minnesota has a Winter Carnival every year. There are ice carving and snow sculpture contests. People carve big statues of cars, buildings, and animals.

This great state has been brought to you by _Nick Nation_

State  **MISSISSIPPI**

Its nickname is ___Magnolia State___

Its capital is ___Jackson___

FAMOUS PERSON

JEFFERSON DAVIS GREW UP IN MISSISSIPPI. DURING THE CIVIL WAR, HE SERVED AS THE PRESIDENT OF THE CONFEDERATE STATES.

MISSISSIPPI RIVER

"MRS. IPPY"

DELTA BLUES

COTTON

TUPELO - ELVIS'S BIRTHPLACE

TOWBOATS

SOYBEANS

PETRIFIED FOREST

JACKSON

VICKSBURG CIVIL WAR BATTLEFIELD

CATFISH

SOUTHERN PLANTATIONS

SHRIMP

GULF COAST BEACHES

The Mississippi River is the western boundary of this state. The soil next to the river is very good for farming. Blues music was started by slaves from Africa who were working in the Mississippi cotton fields. Some famous blues singers from Mississippi were Robert Johnson, Memphis Minnie, and Muddy Waters.

This great state has been brought to you by ___Delron Moore___

State **MISSOURI**

Some people say that people in Missouri don't believe anything until they see it.

Its nickname is **The Show-Me State** ←

Its capital is **Jefferson City** ← Named after President Thomas Jefferson.

Missouri touches eight other states—Iowa, Nebraska, Kansas, Oklahoma, Arkansas, Tennessee, Kentucky, and Illinois. Tennessee is the only other state to touch that many. The Gateway Arch in St. Louis is the tallest monument in the U.S. It looks like a shiny steel upside-down letter U.

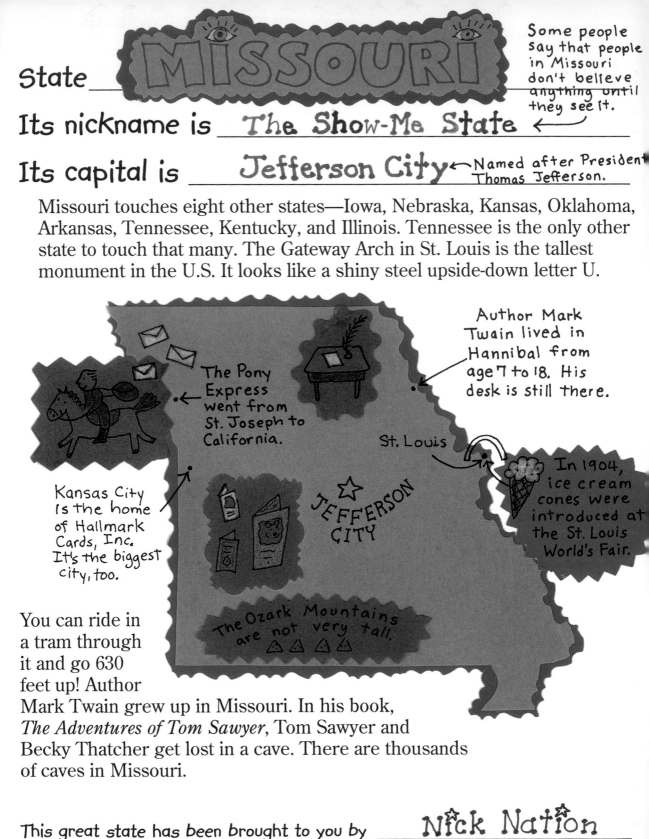

The Pony Express went from St. Joseph to California.

Author Mark Twain lived in Hannibal from age 7 to 18. His desk is still there.

Kansas City is the home of Hallmark Cards, Inc. It's the biggest city, too.

St. Louis

JEFFERSON CITY

In 1904, ice cream cones were introduced at the St. Louis World's Fair.

The Ozark Mountains are not very tall.

You can ride in a tram through it and go 630 feet up! Author Mark Twain grew up in Missouri. In his book, *The Adventures of Tom Sawyer*, Tom Sawyer and Becky Thatcher get lost in a cave. There are thousands of caves in Missouri.

This great state has been brought to you by **Nick Nation**

State **MONTANA**

Its nickname is <u>The Treasure State</u>

Its capital is <u>Helena</u>

A glacier is a mountain of ice floating in a river. *Brrr!* There are 25 glaciers in Glacier National Park!

Glacier National Park

This part of Montana is in the Rocky Mountains.

HELENA ☆

Captain William Clark carved his name on a rock here while he was exploring the West in 1806.

Lewis and Clark

Billings is Montana's biggest city.

Yellowstone River

A city named Butte. It rhymes with "hoot." (My brother says it wrong.)

The top part of Yellowstone National Park is in Montana.

Little Bighorn River

Little Bighorn National Monument

General George Custer fought a battle here with Native Americans in 1876. He lost, so the battlefield is sometimes called Custer's Last Stand.

Montana is called the Treasure State because of its gold, silver, copper, coal, oil, natural gas, and sapphires. But Montana has other kinds of treasures like animals, parks, and mountains. If you like peace and quiet, you might like Montana. There are only six people for every square mile. Montana has more cows than people. I think they should call it Moo-ntana.

MOOOONTANA

This great state has been brought to you by <u>Nick Nation</u>

State **NEBRASKA**

Its nickname is **The Cornhusker State**

Its capital is **Lincoln** ← Named after President Abraham Lincoln.

Yahoo!

These are the biggest sand dunes in North America!

The Sand Hills

Arbor Day began in Nebraska.

The Ak-Sar-Ben (That's Nebraska spelled backwards.) Rodeo is held in Omaha every autumn.

I'm wild about the West!

Omaha is the biggest city in Nebraska.

Highway 80 follows The Oregon Trail somewhat.

Buffalo Bill State Historical Park has a museum with stuff from Buffalo Bill's Wild West Show.

LINCOLN

Whee! The National Museum of Roller Skating is in Lincoln.

Most of Nebraska is in the Great Plains, where it is flat and good for growing crops like corn. There are also lots of cows in Nebraska. If you lined them all up, the cows would go across the USA—two times! In the city of Omaha is the world's largest livestock market. Buffalo Bill's Wild West Show began as a rodeo in Nebraska in 1882. Two years later, Annie Oakley became a star of the show.

This great state has been brought to you by **Nick Nation**

State  **NEVADA**

Its nickname is _The Silver State_

Its capital is _CARSON CITY_

A lot of Nevada is desert, and it rains less there than in any other state. Even so, Nevada has been one of the fastest-growing states with more and more people moving in. Nevada mines silver, copper and turquoise. There are also more than 600 ghost towns near shut-down mines. And then there's Las Vegas with its flashy casinos and neon lights.

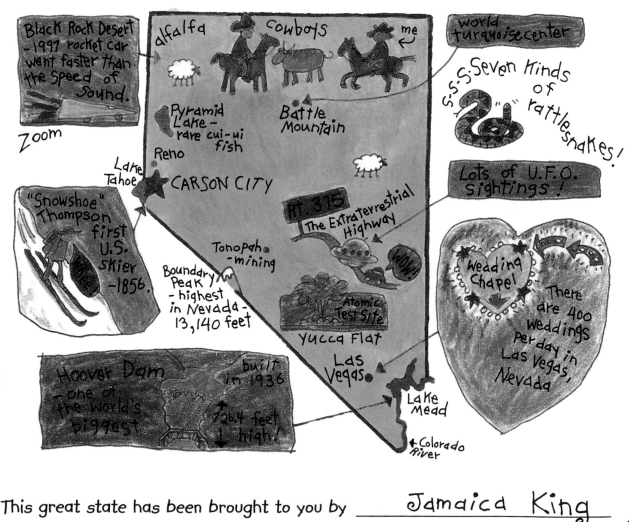

Black Rock Desert -1997 rocket car went faster than the speed of sound. Zoom

alfalfa

cowboys

me

world turquoise center

S-S-S-Seven Kinds of "B" rattlesnakes!

Pyramid Lake - rare cui-ui fish

Battle Mountain

Reno

Lake Tahoe

CARSON CITY

Lots of U.F.O. sightings!

"Snowshoe" Thompson first U.S. skier -1856.

Rt. 375 The Extraterrestrial Highway

WOW!

Tonopah -mining

Boundary Peak - highest in Nevada - 13,140 feet

Wedding Chapel

There are 400 weddings per day in Las Vegas, Nevada

Atomic Test Site

Yucca Flat

Las Vegas

Hoover Dam - one of the world's biggest

built in 1936

726.4 feet high!

Lake Mead

Colorado River

This great state has been brought to you by _Jamaica King_

State 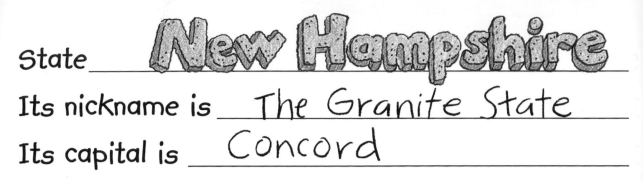 **New Hampshire**

Its nickname is _The Granite State_

Its capital is _Concord_

One of the thirteen original colonies, New Hampshire was the first to declare its independence from England, several weeks before the Declaration of Independence was signed on July 4, 1776.

We get granite, rocks and gravel from New Hampshire.

The first potato planted in the U.S. was planted in New Hampshire in 1719. I love fries!

Mount Washington is the highest point in New England at 6,288 feet.

Lake Winnipesaukee

Concord

Peterborough Home of the first free public library in 1833.

Portsmouth

Portsmouth has been known for shipbuilding since 1630. Today the shipyard builds and repairs submarines.

This great state has been brought to you by _Joe_

State **New Jersey**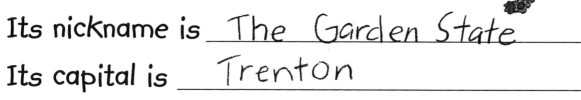

Its nickname is The Garden State

Its capital is Trenton

New Jersey is called the Garden State because more than half of the state is still open land with farms, woods, marshes, and beaches. The New Jersey shoreline, with its beautiful beaches, is a very popular tourist area.

The honeybee is the state bug.

Thomas Edison worked in Menlo Park.

Newark.

Elizabeth.

A large seaport is located in Newark and Elizabeth.

New Jersey produces two-thirds of the world's eggplants.

Trenton

Eggplant parmesan is delicious!

Atlantic City

Atlantic City is where the street names for the boardgame Monopoly come from. It is also the home of the Miss America Pageant.

This great state has been brought to you by ___Joe___

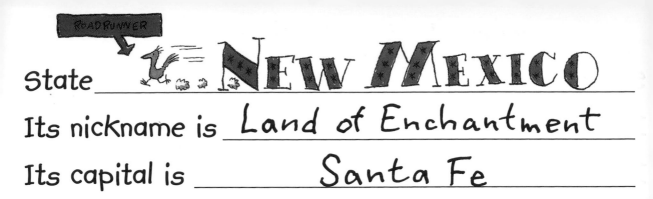

State **NEW MEXICO**

Its nickname is _Land of Enchantment_

Its capital is _Santa Fe_

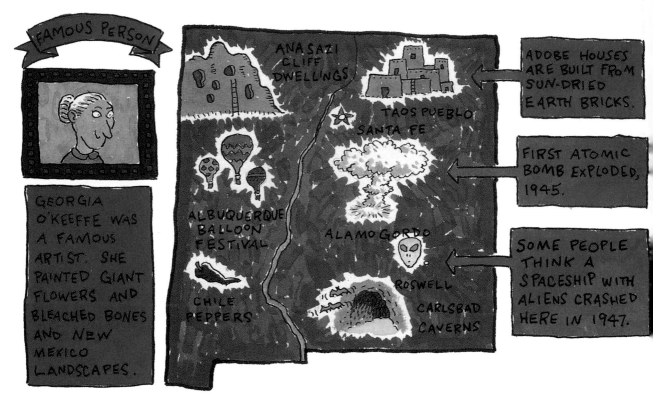

FAMOUS PERSON

GEORGIA O'KEEFFE WAS A FAMOUS ARTIST. SHE PAINTED GIANT FLOWERS AND BLEACHED BONES AND NEW MEXICO LANDSCAPES.

ANASAZI CLIFF DWELLINGS

TAOS PUEBLO

SANTA FE

ALBUQUERQUE BALLOON FESTIVAL

CHILE PEPPERS

ALAMOGORDO

ROSWELL

CARLSBAD CAVERNS

ADOBE HOUSES ARE BUILT FROM SUN-DRIED EARTH BRICKS.

FIRST ATOMIC BOMB EXPLODED, 1945.

SOME PEOPLE THINK A SPACESHIP WITH ALIENS CRASHED HERE IN 1947.

Some people don't know that Santa Fe is the oldest capital city in the United States. It was founded by Spanish explorers in 1610. New Mexico also has one of the oldest towns in the U.S. It is called Acoma Pueblo, and people have lived there since about 1075! The symbol on the New Mexico state flag is the sun sign of the Zia Pueblo people. It stands for happiness and prosperity.

This great state has been brought to you by _Delron Moore_

State  **NEW YORK**

Its nickname is _The Empire State_

Its capital is _Albany_

Between 1892 and 1954, about 12 million immigrants came to the United States through Ellis Island. People could see the Statue of Liberty from there. The United States is called a melting pot because we are a country of people from all over the world, all melted into one nation.

New York has more than 18,000 dairy farms.

Finger Lakes

Albany ★

Catskill Mountains

The first macaroni factory in the U.S. was in Brooklyn.

New York City

This great state has been brought to you by _Joe_

State **North Carolina**

Its nickname is **Tar Heel State**

Its capital is **Raleigh**

North Carolina is a southeastern state with beautiful beaches in the east and mountains in the west.

1ST Orville and Wilbur Wright took their 1st flight on Dec. 17, 1903 from Kitty Hawk.

Kitty Hawk

Fine furniture is made here.

Lots of ships got lost after crashing into the Outer Banks.

FUN FACT Gold!

The fact that I like the best is about GOLD! In 1799, a farmer's twelve-year-old son found a large yellow rock. The farmer used it for a doorstop until he found out it was gold! He quit farming and went on to find more gold. Today you can visit the Reed Gold Mine.

Tori

This great state has been brought to you by _____

NORTH DAKOTA

State _____

Its nickname is ___The Flickertail State___ *4 nicknames!*

Its capital is ___Bismarck___
or Sioux State
or Peace Garden State
or Rough Rider State

North Dakota is the state with the fewest trees so most of the land is good for farming or ranching. Its farms grow the most durum wheat in the U.S. Durum wheat is used to make noodles. Bonanzaville is a pioneer village you can visit. Every June, people there ride 100 miles in covered wagons to celebrate the pioneers. The Badlands is a part of the state where you can see big twisted rocks that are blue, pink, yellow. It got its name because the Sioux tribe thought the land was hard to live on.

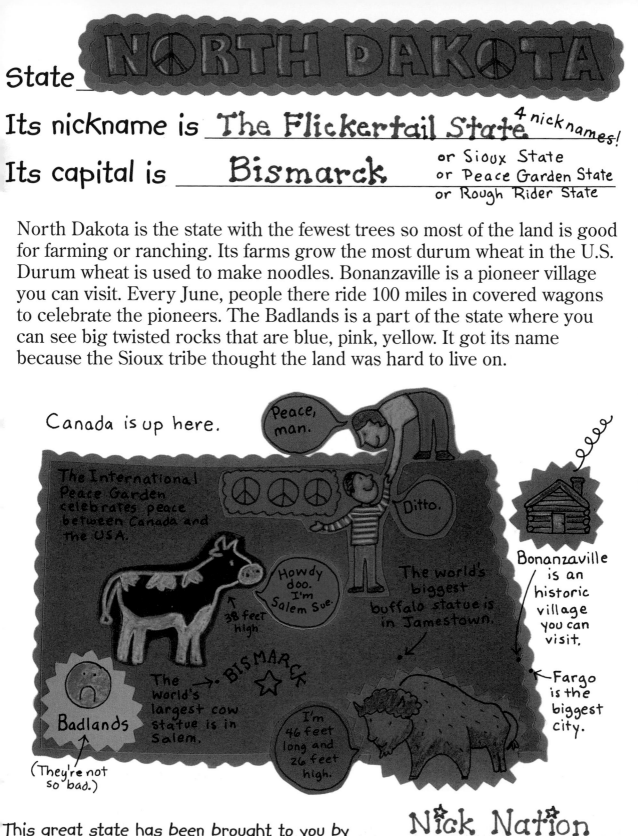

Canada is up here.

Peace, man.

The International Peace Garden celebrates peace between Canada and the USA.

Ditto.

Howdy doo. I'm Salem Sue.

↑ 38 feet high

The world's biggest buffalo statue is in Jamestown.

Bonanzaville is an historic village you can visit.

BISMARCK ☆

The world's largest cow statue is in Salem.

I'm 46 feet long and 26 feet high.

Badlands

(They're not so bad.)

←Fargo is the biggest city.

This great state has been brought to you by ___Nick Nation___

41

State **OHiO**

A Buckeye is a tree that grows in Ohio.

Its nickname is The Buckeye State

Its capital is Columbus

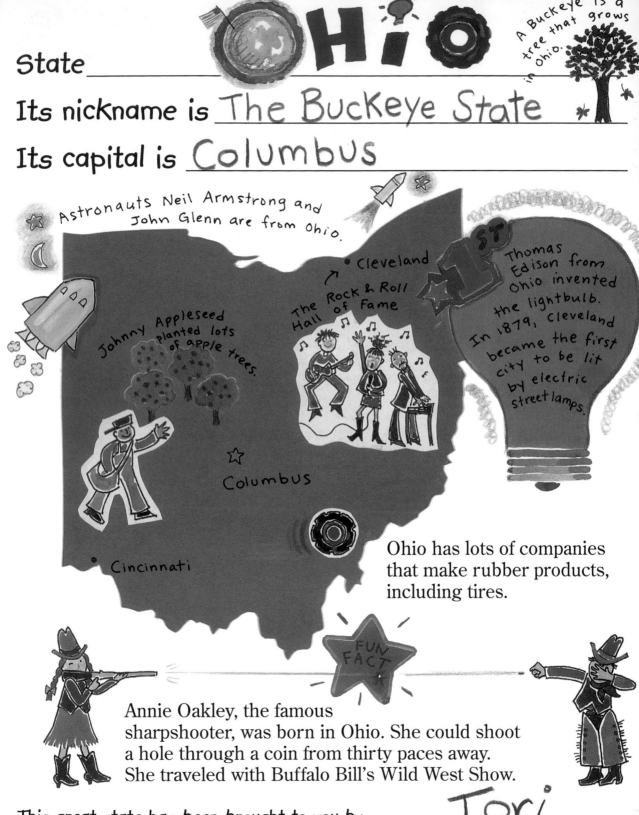

Astronauts Neil Armstrong and John Glenn are from Ohio.

Cleveland

The Rock & Roll Hall of Fame

Johnny Appleseed planted lots of apple trees.

1ST

Thomas Edison from Ohio invented the lightbulb. In 1879, Cleveland became the first city to be lit by electric street lamps.

Columbus

Cincinnati

Ohio has lots of companies that make rubber products, including tires.

FUN FACT

Annie Oakley, the famous sharpshooter, was born in Ohio. She could shoot a hole through a coin from thirty paces away. She traveled with Buffalo Bill's Wild West Show.

This great state has been brought to you by ___ Tori

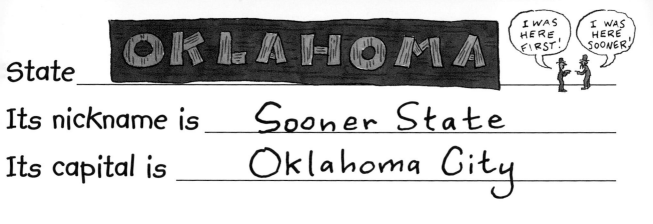

State OKLAHOMA

Its nickname is Sooner State

Its capital is Oklahoma City

In 1830 the government forced Native Americans to leave their lands in the southeastern U.S. and move to Oklahoma. Thousands died during the march. It was called the Trail of Tears.

Oklahoma is called the Sooner State because of a race for land in 1889. There were two million acres to be settled. Whoever got to a piece of land first won it. The race was supposed to start at noon on April 22, but some settlers snuck in early. They were called "Sooners."

This great state has been brought to you by  Delron Moore

State  **OREGON**

Its nickname is ___The Beaver State___

Its capital is ___SALEM___

In the 1840s, pioneers in covered wagons came to Oregon to become farmers in the Willamette Valley. Today Oregon still grows lots of wheat, grapes, apples, pears, and hazelnuts. But Oregon is best known for its forests. Half the state is trees! Lots of Christmas trees are grown there. Oregonians care a lot about the environment. It's a beautiful state, and they want to keep it that way!

Chinook Salmon

Tuna

Sea otter

Track capital of the world.

Coos Bay

Big lumber port

The rare spotted owl can only live in old, thick dark woods.

Astoria

fish ladders

Portland -city of roses

SALEM

Eugene

Timberrr!

Mt. McLoughlin

The Columbia River has the strongest current in the U.S.

Columbia River

←me

year round winter sports

Mt. Hood

WILLAMETTE VALLEY

CASCADE MOUNTAINS

Paul Bunyan- folk hero

Crater Lake

deepest lake in the U.S. (1,932 ft.) and one of the world's bluest.

Appaloosa ponies- The Nez Percé Indians first bred them.

Snake River

wild horses

wheat

cattle

grasslands

This great state has been brought to you by ___Jamaica King___

State **Pennsylvania**

Its nickname is _Keystone State_

Its capital is _Harrisburg_

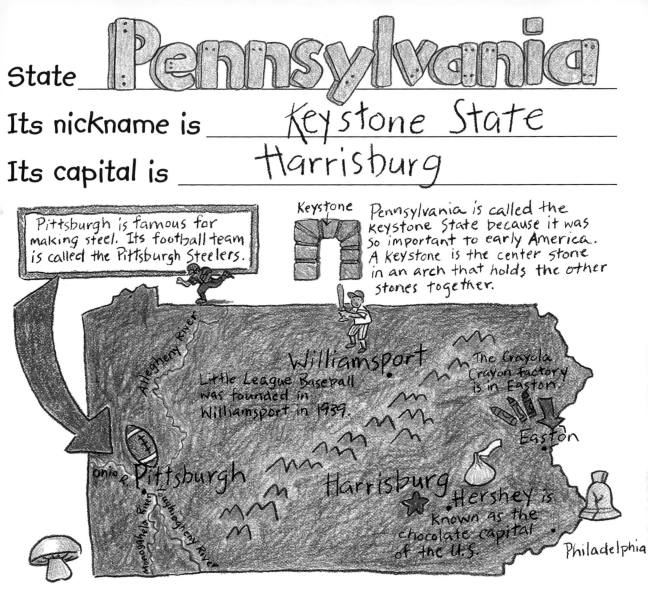

Pittsburgh is famous for making steel. Its football team is called the Pittsburgh Steelers.

Keystone

Pennsylvania is called the Keystone State because it was so important to early America. A keystone is the center stone in an arch that holds the other stones together.

Williamsport

Little League Baseball was founded in Williamsport in 1939.

The Crayola Crayon factory is in Easton.

Easton

Allegheny River

Ohio R.

Monongahela River

Youghiogheny River

Pittsburgh

Harrisburg

Hershey is known as the chocolate capital of the U.S.

Philadelphia

Pennsylvania produces more mushrooms than any other state.

Mushrooms are great on pizza!

Pennsylvania is named after William Penn, who was granted the colony in 1681. Its most famous city is Philadelphia, which is where the Declaration of Independence was signed on July 4, 1776. It is also the home of the Liberty Bell. Benjamin Franklin lived in Philadelphia for many years. In 1754, he drew the first cartoon to appear in an American newspaper.

This great state has been brought to you by _Joe_

45

State  **Rhode Island**

Its nickname is __The Ocean State__

Its capital is __Providence__

The official name of Rhode Island is The State of Rhode Island and Providence Plantations. That is an awfully long name for the smallest state. Rhode Island is 1,045 square miles. You could put 547 Rhode Islands inside Alaska.

Providence

The Rhode Island red hen is the state bird.

Narragansett Bay

Rhode Island is known for making silverware.

Narragansett Indian Reservation is the burial ground of many chiefs.

Newport

One of the first circuses in the U.S. was in Newport.

Block Island is nine miles offshore and was once a favorite hideout for pirates. There are lots of shipwrecks near its shores.

This great state has been brought to you by __Joe__

46

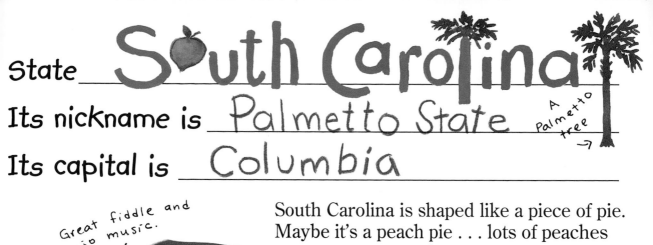

State **South Carolina**

Its nickname is **Palmetto State**

A Palmetto tree →

Its capital is **Columbia**

Great fiddle and banjo music.

South Carolina is shaped like a piece of pie. Maybe it's a peach pie . . . lots of peaches are grown here.

Blue Ridge Mountains

South Carolina is known for its beautiful beaches. Lots of people vacation here... including ME!

Columbia ☆

South Carolina became the first state to break away from the U.S., which led to the Civil War.

Sweetgrass basket-making has been a tradition for more than three hundred years.

Myrtle Beach

Charleston •

The Civil War (1861-65) started at Fort Sumter in Charleston Harbor.

FUN FACT

Magnolia Plantation and Gardens in Charleston features a seventeenth-century Southern mansion surrounded by America's oldest garden.

1ST

The Charleston Museum, founded in 1773, was the first museum in the United States.

This great state has been brought to you by **Tori**

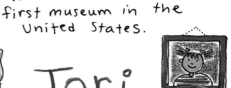

47

State **SOUTH DAKOTA**

Its nickname is <u>The Sunshine State</u>

Its capital is **Pierre**

or Mt. Rushmore State

Dakota means "friend" in Sioux.

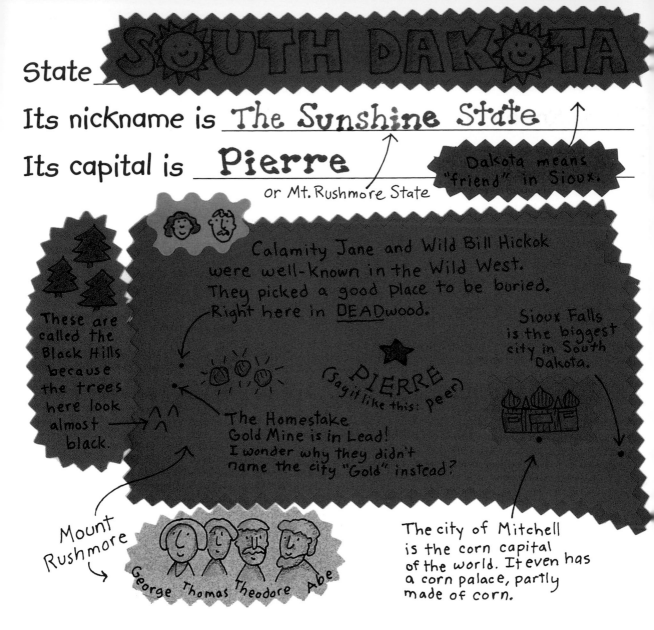

Calamity Jane and Wild Bill Hickok were well-known in the Wild West. They picked a good place to be buried. Right here in <u>DEAD</u>wood.

These are called the Black Hills because the trees here look almost black.

The Homestake Gold Mine is in Lead! I wonder why they didn't name the city "Gold" instead?

PIERRE (Say it like this: peer)

Sioux Falls is the biggest city in South Dakota.

Mount Rushmore

George Thomas Theodore Abe

The city of Mitchell is the corn capital of the world. It even has a corn palace, partly made of corn.

Mount Rushmore is the biggest sculpture in the world. It is made of granite and took 360 men fourteen years to carve. It is a statue of the faces of four U.S. presidents: George Washington, Thomas Jefferson, Theodore Roosevelt, and Abraham Lincoln. Their heads are six stories high. Their noses are 20 feet long. (If they had boogers, imagine how big they would be!) A statue of Sioux Chief Crazy Horse is being carved in the Black Hills. When it's finished, it'll be bigger than Mount Rushmore.

This great state has been brought to you by **Nick Nation**

State 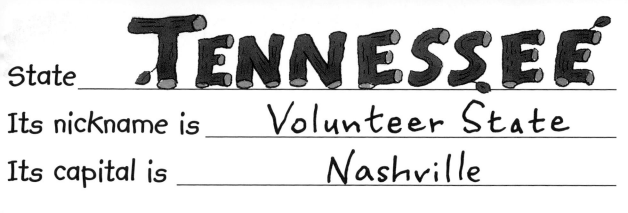 **TENNESSEE**

Its nickname is ___Volunteer State___

Its capital is ___Nashville___

Eastern Tennessee has the Smoky Mountains; from a look-out point you can see seven states! Middle Tennessee has Nashville, the home of Country and Western music. And western Tennessee has Memphis, the birthplace of rock 'n' roll. Tennessee has had three U.S. presidents—Andrew Jackson, James K. Polk, and Andrew Johnson. And two "kings"—Davy Crockett, "the King of the Wild Frontier," and Elvis Presley, "the King of Rock 'n' Roll."

NASHVILLE
GIBSON GUITARS
POULTRY
GRACELAND (ELVIS'S HOUSE)
MEMPHIS
FedEx
HOGS
GRAND OLE OPRY
LOOKOUT MOUNTAIN
TENNESSEE WALKING HORSE
KNOXVILLE
DAVY CROCKETT BIRTHPLACE
SMOKY MOUNTAINS

FAMOUS PERSON

ELVIS PRESLEY WAS ONE OF THE FIRST ROCK 'N' ROLL SINGERS. YOU CAN VISIT HIS MANSION IN MEMPHIS AND SEE HIS COLLECTION OF COOL CARS.

This great state has been brought to you by ___Delron Moore___

State _____

Its nickname is __Lone Star State__

Its capital is __Austin__

FAMOUS PERSON

GEORGE W. BUSH, 43RD PRESIDENT OF THE U.S.A.

COWGIRLS

COMPARE THE SIZE OF TEXAS WITH THE SIZE OF CONNECTICUT!

CONNECTICUT

PARIS

DALLAS

ARMADILLOS

FT. WORTH

WEST TEXAS

COWBOYS

BLUE BONNETS (STATE FLOWER)

BIG BEND NATIONAL PARK

AUSTIN

OIL

JOHNSON SPACE CENTER

HOUSTON

LONGHORN CATTLE

THE ALAMO

GULF OF MEXICO

WHOOPING CRANES

SHRIMP BOATS

Texas is famous for oil wells, cows, and cowboys. After the Civil War, one out of every three cowboys was either African-American or Mexican! Texas is also famous for chili and other Tex-Mex food. Tex-Mex food is Mexican food cooked Texas style. To make Wylene's Texas Cheese Bread: Mix a small can of chopped green chilies with one-half cup of mayonnaise and two cups of grated jack cheese. Spread on sliced bread and then ask a grown-up to put it in the oven and bake for ten minutes at 350 degrees. YAHEE!

This great state has been brought to you by __Delron Moore__

State  **UTAH**

Its nickname is **The Beehive State**

Its capital is **SALT LAKE CITY**

Brigham Young led the Mormon people across the country to Utah. They settled at Salt Lake. Between 1847 and 1877, the settlers started 350 other Mormon colonies! They worked like bees, and that's why Utah is called the "Beehive State." Utah is very dry, but it has some rivers that are great for rafting. In the mountains there's snow and skiing. There are also weird and colorful rock formations and canyons in Zion National Park and Bryce Canyon.

me

It's so salty you float really high. It's hard to swim underwater - You bob up!

Great Salt Lake

Promontory Point

Bonneville Salt Flats

600 mph!

SALT LAKE CITY

The Golden Spike — In 1869 Union Pacific and Central Pacific Railroads meet here — the first cross-country railroad.

Uinta Mountains

Spotted skunk - stands on it's head!

FOSSIL

Provo

Steel center of the west

Desert

Dinosaur National Monument

Philo T. Farnsworth, father of television, born here. (1906-71)

Price - coal

3,000 Mormon settlers pulled wooden handcarts across the plains, 1856-60.

Zion Narrows Canyon is so deep and narrow you can see stars from the bottom in daytime.

Beaver

copper mines

Zion National Park

Capitol Reef National

Bryce Canyon

Moab

mountain biking

Lake Powell

Rainbow Bridge National Monument

highest natural arch

This great state has been brought to you by **Jamaica King**

51

State **Vermont**

Its nickname is ___Green Mountain State___

Its capital is ___Montpelier___

Ben & Jerrys Ice Cream company gives leftovers to farmers who feed it to their hogs. The hogs like every flavor except Mint Chocolate Cookie.

Montpelier

It takes 40 gallons of maple tree sap to make one gallon of maple syrup.

Vermont is the largest producer of maple syrup in the United States!

Beautiful!

Vermont has the smallest population of any state east of the Mississippi River, and Montpelier is the smallest state capital in the U.S., with only about 8,000 people. Forests cover 80% of the state. Thousands of tourists visit Vermont in the fall to see the leaves on the trees change colors.

Joe

This great state has been brought to you by ___Joe___

State **VIRGINIA**

Its nickname is Mother of Presidents

Its capital is Richmond

Eight U.S. presidents were born in Virginia, including George Washington and Thomas Jefferson.

In the 1700s, Blackbeard the pirate buried treasure along the eastern coast. People are still hunting for it today!

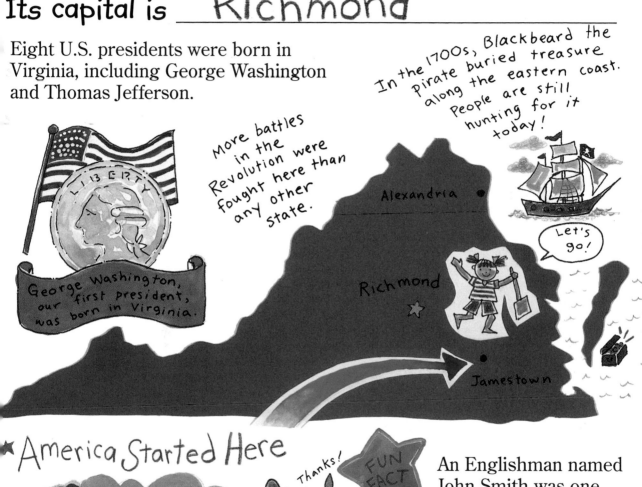

More battles in the Revolution were fought here than any other state.

George Washington, our first president, was born in Virginia.

Alexandria

Richmond

Let's go!

Jamestown

★ America Started Here

1ST

The first permanent English colony was settled in Jamestown in 1607.

Thanks!

FUN FACT

An Englishman named John Smith was one of the first settlers. He was captured by the Powhatan Indians. Pocahontas, the chief's daughter, saved John Smith from being killed.

This great state has been brought to you by ___Tori___

State  **WASHINGTON**

Its nickname is _The Evergreen State_

Its capital is _OLYMPIA_

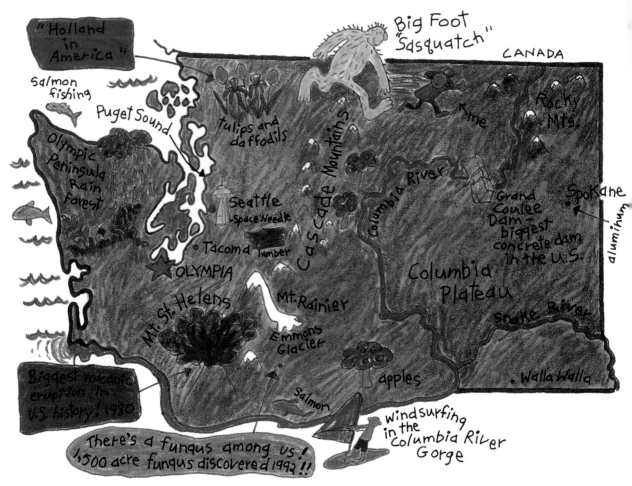

"Holland in America"

Big Foot "Sasquatch"

CANADA

Salmon fishing

Puget Sound

tulips and daffodils

Cascade Mountains

time

Rocky Mts.

Olympic Peninsula Rain Forest

Seattle
Space Needle

Columbia River

Grand Coulee Dam - biggest concrete dam in the U.S.

Spokane

aluminum

Tacoma lumber

OLYMPIA

Columbia Plateau

Mt. St. Helens

Mt. Rainier

Emmons Glacier

Snake River

Biggest volcanic eruption in U.S. history! 1980

apples

Walla Walla

Salmon

windsurfing in the Columbia River Gorge

There's a fungus among us! 1,500 acre fungus discovered 1992!!

Washington is the only state named for a president. The western part of the state is rainy—some places get 180 inches a year! But, on the other side of the Cascade Mountains, it's as dry as a desert. With watering, crops like wheat and pears grow there. Washington is the top apple grower in the world.

This great state has been brought to you by _Jamaica King_

State **West Virginia**

Its nickname is The Mountain State

Its capital is Charleston

A Big Split

West Virginia used to be part of Virginia. It split off from the eastern part of the state in 1863 because settlers in western Virginia were against slavery. Many battles of the Civil War were fought in West Virginia.

The entire state of West Virginia lies in the Appalachian Mountain system. That's why West Virginia is nicknamed "The Mountain State."

Come to West Virginia to go hiking, rock climbing and rafting.

There's hardly any flat land in West Virginia!

1ST

Chuck Yeager, from Myra, was the first person to travel faster than the speed of sound in 1947.

Charleston

West Virginia has lots of coal mines.

FUN FACT

If you have marbles, there is a good chance they were made in West Virginia, which has many glass plants.

This great state has been brought to you by Tori

WISCONSIN

State _____

Its nickname is <u>The Badger State</u>

Its capital is ____<u>Madison</u> (Named for President James Madison.)

Bloomer is the jump rope capital of the world. Kids there enter ten-second speed jumping contests. One kid jumped 58 times in 10 seconds!

MOO

Magician Harry Houdini grew up in Appleton. He could escape from handcuffs and locked boxes.

I'm flying in!

Oshkosh

And I'm wearing overalls.

Ringling Bros. started their circus in the town of Baraboo. The Circus World Museum is here. It has circus wagons and carousels.

MADISON ☆

Milwaukee is ↗ the biggest city.

Say cheese,

Cheese!

Wisconsin makes the most cheese of any state: two billion pounds a year. More than a million cows live there. So lots of milk and butter also come from Wisconsin. The city of Oshkosh is famous for a company that makes overalls. Every summer at the Oshkosh Fly-In, 10,000 small airplanes fly in for this celebration.

This great state has been brought to you by _____ Nick Nation

State

Its nickname is ___The Cowboy State; The Equality State___

Its capital is ___CHEYENNE___

Wyoming used to be part of the Wild West, a land of cowboys and Indians and rustlers and rodeos. Today most of Wyoming is still grazing land for cattle and sheep, though there are lots of oil wells and coal mines. Wyoming has the biggest elk herds in the world, but there are fewer people there than any other state. In 1869 Wyoming was the first state to let women vote because they thought it might make more people want to live there. (I guess that didn't work.) In 1872 Yellowstone Park became the first national park.

The Windiest State

First National Monument-1906

YOW!

Mr. T - The greatest bucking bull - threw 180 cowboys in 5 years in the 1980's!

Most fossilized fish in the world

Yellowstone National Park
Old Faithful
Great camping!
Dayton-First Dude Ranch
Devil's Tower
Grizzly Bears
Bridger-Teton National Forest
K me
Jackson Hole
Rocky Mountains
Cowboys
Prairie Dogs
Give me a home where the buffalo roam ... and the deer and the antelope play...
Casper-oil capital of the Rockies
Fossil Butte
Laramie
CHEYENNE
The 10-Gallon Cowboy hat - invented by Max Meyer

This great state has been brought to you by ___Jamaica King___

City

State

WASHINGTON

District of Columbia

Its nickname is ___Nation's Capital; D.C.; The District___

Its ~~capital~~ is ___Capital of the U.S. !___

The President lives here.

U.S. money is printed in D.C and so are stamps.

THE VIETNAM VETERANS MEMORIAL

ROCK Creek Park

THE NATIONAL ZOO

THE LIBRARY OF CONGRESS The world's biggest library — 34½ million books.

THE LINCOLN MEMORIAL

pandas

me ↓

THE WHITE HOUSE

THE U.S. CAPITOL BUILDING

Congress meets here.

MALL

the Smithsonian Museum is on the Mall.

THE WASHINGTON MONUMENT — the city's tallest building. When the temperature outside rises suddenly, it rains INSIDE!

3,000 cherry trees grow around the Tidal Basin. The trees were a present from Japan.

Potomac River

THE JEFFERSON MEMORIAL

Duke Ellington, jazzman, was born here.

Washington, D.C., isn't in any state, because it's the capital of the whole country! It is the city where our government works. Until 1800 Washington was just a swamp. Now it has beautiful buildings and monuments. In 1963 my aunt saw Martin Luther King, Jr., give his "I have a dream" speech near the Lincoln Memorial. When I visit my cousins in D.C., we always go to the Smithsonian museums. I saw George Washington's false teeth there.

This great state has been brought to you by ___Jamaica King___

The United States Flag
by Joe

The first U.S. flags all had 13 stars and 13 stripes, one for each of the original thirteen states. The colors were red, white and blue, but there weren't any rules for how the stars and stripes should be arranged.

Later on, when a new state joined the union one more star and one more stripe were added to the flag. This version of the flag was flying when Francis Scott Key wrote "The Star-Spangled Banner."

Then, in 1818, it was decided to stick with 13 stripes. And in the blue box, there would be one star for each state.

Flag of 1812

The Flag since 1960

HOW OUR

THE UNITED STATES IN 1788

IN 1788 THE UNITED STATES AND ITS TERRITORIES SPREAD FROM THE ATLANTIC OCEAN TO THE MISSISSIPPI RIVER.

BABY SAM

THE UNITED STATES IN 1819

GIVEN UP BY GREAT BRITAIN IN 1818

THE LOUISIANA PURCHASE WAS THE NAME GIVEN TO THE LAND BOUGHT FROM FRANCE IN 1803 FOR 15 MILLION DOLLARS.

SPAIN GAVE UP FLORIDA TO THE U.S. IN 1803.

TEEN SAM

COUNTRY GREW

THE UNITED STATES IN 1845

THE REPUBLIC OF TEXAS WON ITS INDEPENDENCE FROM MEXICO IN 1836, AND WAS A SEPARATE COUNTRY FOR ALMOST TEN YEARS. IN 1845 IT BECAME PART OF THE U.S.

YOUNG MAN SAM

THE UNITED STATES IN 1900

HAWAII WAS ADDED IN 1898.

IN THE OREGON TREATY OF 1846, THE U.S.-CANADA BORDER WAS FIXED AT THE 49TH PARALLEL.

ALASKA WAS BOUGHT FROM RUSSIA IN 1867.

THE MEXICAN CESSION 1848: LAND WON FROM MEXICO IN THE MEXICAN-AMERICAN WAR.

THE GADSDEN PURCHASE, 1854: LAND BOUGHT FROM MEXICO FOR TEN MILLION DOLLARS.

UNCLE SAM

Delron Moore

1

George Washington
1789-1797
Born in Virginia

I was the first!

I'm president now!

Our Presidents
by Joe

44

Barack Obama
2009-
Born in Hawaii

2

John Adams
1797-1801
Born in Massachusetts

3

Thomas Jefferson
1801-1809
Born in Virginia

4

James Madison
1809-1817
Born in Virginia

5

James Monroe
1817-1825
Born in Virginia

6

John Quincy Adams
1825-1829
Born in Massachusetts

7

Andrew Jackson
1829-1837
Born in South Carolina

8

Martin Van Buren
1837-1841
Born in New York

9

William Henry Harrison
1841
Born in Virginia

10

John Tyler
1841-1845
Born in Virginia

11

James K. Polk
1845-1849
Born in North Carolina

12

Zachary Taylor
1849-1850
Born in Virginia

13

Millard Fillmore
1850-1853
Born in New York

14

Franklin Pierce
1853-1857
Born in New Hampshire

15

James Buchanan
1857-1861
Born in Pennsylvania

16

Abraham Lincoln
1861-1865
Born in Kentucky

17

Andrew Johnson
1865-1869
Born in North Carolina

18

Ulysses S. Grant
1869-1877
Born in Ohio

19

Rutherford B. Hayes
1877-1881
Born in Ohio

20	**21**	**22**	**23**	**24**	**25**
James A. Garfield 1881 Born in Ohio	Chester A. Arthur 1881–1885 Born in Vermont	Grover Cleveland 1885–1889 Born in New Jersey	Benjamin Harrison 1889–1893 Born in Ohio	Grover Cleveland 1893–1897 Born in New Jersey	William McKinley 1897–1901 Born in Ohio
26	**27**	**28**	**29**	**30**	**31**
Theodore Roosevelt 1901–1909 Born in New York	William H. Taft 1909–1913 Born in Ohio	Woodrow Wilson 1913–1921 Born in Virginia	Warren G. Harding 1921–1923 Born in Ohio	Calvin Coolidge 1923–1929 Born in Vermont	Herbert Hoover 1929–1933 Born in Iowa
32	**33**	**34**	**35**	**36**	**37**
Franklin D. Roosevelt 1933–1945 Born in New York	Harry S. Truman 1945–1953 Born in Missouri	Dwight D. Eisenhower 1953–1961 Born in Texas	John F. Kennedy 1961–1963 Born in Massachusetts	Lyndon B. Johnson 1963–1969 Born in Texas	Richard M. Nixon 1969–1974 Born in California
38	**39**	**40**	**41**	**42**	**43**
Gerald R. Ford 1974–1977 Born in Nebraska	Jimmy Carter 1977–1981 Born in Georgia	Ronald Reagan 1981–1989 Born in Illinois	George Bush 1989–1993 Born in Massachusetts	William Jefferson Clinton 1993–2001 Born in Arkansas	George W. Bush 2001–2009 Born in Connecticut

BIBLIOGRAPHY

Here is a list of books we used for our report.

Stuck on the U.S.A. by Gus Alavezos (published by Grosset & Dunlap)

Scholastic Atlas of the United States by David Rubel
(published by Scholastic Reference)

Wish You Were Here by Kathleen Krull (published by Bantam Books)

National Geographic Picture Atlas of Our Fifty States
(published by National Geographic Book Society)

World Book Encyclopedia (published by World Book Inc.)

Lonely Planet Guides (published by Lonely Planet)

Celebrate the 50 States by Loreen Leedy
(published by Holiday House)

For some states, we got information by writing to the state's Chamber of Commerce (that's a special office that has lots of facts and information about the state). And we used the website www.50states.com. Also, we went to each state's website. You can find them by going to www.usa.gov. There are special websites for each state that are just for kids!

> Dear Team USA,
> I learned so much from your report. It looks as if you all had fun working together. On my next vacation, I am driving across the country. I am taking your report with me!
>
> Ms. Brandt